TH
Journey
Through

Geraldine Yount

Cover Art: Jessica Yount

If we ever get the drift of how much God loves us, we will understand how much he wants to share our earth journey. If we just read His word and use it as our guide in life, things turn out so much better. It's like we are living in the Garden of Eden again. Well, not entirely, because in this fallen world we will have tribulation, but be of good cheer for He has overcome the world. Still a fallen world though.

I'm a little annoyed at Adam for turning over the keys of earth to Satan, but I'm so grateful that Jesus came to save us from our sins and get the keys back.

Is every day going to be roses? Probably not, but there is always a flower blooming somewhere in our life. We just have to find it. Don't ever give up. Always look for God's best for you and send your angels out to minister for you. They can only hearken to God's word. It's like a computer program — only works one way. No need to try to change it, like gravity, always gonna work the same way

When you start walking daily with Jesus, other people aren't going to be as excited as you are. It's like a special students program-IEP – Individualized Educational Programs. That's what God has for you. (and you are His special student. We all are.) What makes sense to you probably won't to someone else. But just hang in there – God has a plan for your life.

We all travel at our own speed. I'm convinced that what we don't learn here, we have to learn there. But that's just my thought — so I'm studying hard for my final exam.

God loves you so much that he wants to show out for you and bless you and just let you know that He's around. Some call these coincidences. I call them God-incidences. This book is about my own personal experiences. You have some too, I know you do.

Some of the stories in this book seem similar and have similar themes, but I have been faithful to record them exactly as God gave them to me. I hope they bless you.

"Bless the Lord, o my soul and all that is within me, bless His holy name, and forget none of His benefits...." Psalm 103:1, 2

"I will not leave you comfortless; I will come to you." John 14:18

MORNING GLORIES

I love Morning Glories with their heart-shaped leaves and profusion of multicolored delicate flowers. Thus, I was very sad the year that I failed to replant along the backyard fence. For several years, I had scooted along the fence, sitting in the rich brown earth to tuck the small seeds securely into the ground. During the summer, which I hate, my reward was getting up each morning to the glories of the morning. It always made me smile.

But alas, this year, my husband, without malice or intent, had sprayed Round-up along that fence line that before had provided a beautiful place to linger over first coffee. I thought I could handle it, but during the heat of my morning-glory-less Summer, I became a Morning Glory junkie and begged my grandson, the landscaper, to please go locate some plants for Grammy. I also poured over the internet, but none was to be had. I literally was mourning for my morning-glories — no pun intended.

But God had another plan, as He always does. About the middle of September, I thought I saw, yes I DID SEE some heart-shaped leaves crawling up that western fence. I wonderingly watched as the leaves turned into vines and displayed themselves along the naked fence. I couldn't believe my eyes. It wasn't too much longer, when a tiny bloom appeared. Intrigued, I visited this wonderful gift from God first thing each and every morning to see what would happen next.

One day I counted 4 plants, 10 purple blooms and 1 white bloom. God never does things small. He always does them abundantly.

Frost was late in our part of the country this year and the plants kept me thrilled each morning with new blossoms up unto the early part of December. At last, the vines lay shriveled on the fence but never in my heart.

Now could I have made it through that year without Morning-Glories? Of course I could have. But the Beautiful God of us all, didn't see it that way. He looked down and saw my situation and wanted to bless me just because of who He is. We're all His favorite children. He wants to bless you too.

And guess what? That was last Summer. This spring those magic plants just went right ahead and reseeded themselves even before I could plant more.

"To appoint unto them that mourn in Zion, to give unto them a garland for ashes, the oil of joy for mourning, the garment of praise for the spirit of heaviness; that they may be called trees of Righteousness, the planting of Jehovah, that he may be glorified." Isaiah 61: 1-3

"Consider the lilies, how they grow; they neither toil nor spin..." Luke 12:27

I DIDN'T KNOW UMBRELLAS COULD FLY

When I returned home from shopping, I started down our long driveway, which gave me a wide view of the roof. Something clearly was amiss, and what to my surprise, I saw the open deck umbrella had been blown by some unknown strong force and was sitting squarely atop of that roof.

Now, how does one get an umbrella down with no access to the roof or a very tall ladder? Since I was home alone for a few days, I went inside to pray about and ponder over this matter.

No distinct answer came and as I left home the next morning, Mr. Umbrella was smiling down at me from his lofty height. I almost felt him waving goodbye as I left.

However, when I got back home, THERE IT WAS! Apparently, the high-flung umbrella had been lifted, still open, still intact, as if gently carried down by angels, and plopped right in the middle of the driveway so I'd be sure to see it.

God never ceases to amaze me. I had a problem. He stepped in and solved it. Then I had no problem. A small problem, granted, but nothing is too small nor too large for God.

"Our help is in the name of the Lord, the maker of heaven and earth." Psalm 124:8

"For nothing will be impossible with God." Luke 1:37

THE RIGHT PLACE, THE RIGHT TIME

Washington Road in our town is a route to be reckoned with. They used to print bumper stickers with the slogan "Pray for Me, I Drive on Washington Road." Unfortunately, it is a main thoroughfare through our town and onward to other places. Unfortunately, our business is located on this street. But, fortunately, they are widening the street, which means they are right now unfortunately, narrowing the street due to construction.

It was in this setting that I was returning from my favorite shopping mall, and proceeding to travel down Washington Road. When I got to a not-so-congested part, I could see ahead that the cars were at least 50 deep. It was quick decision time

"Lord, which way?"

I felt impressed to turn left at the light, get off Washington Road and go the long way around to the small restaurant with great southern vegetables that I could gather up, haul back home, and pretend I'm a great cook. Oh yeah, my husband knows the difference. I'm not that great of a cook I can sing about it, I can write about it, but a gourmet cook, I am not.

So, I veered off to the left and then right to travel along Belair Rd to my delicious destination. As I got back on another not-so-congested part of Washington Rd, I saw coming towards me a police car, blue lights flashing. I traveled another mile and another police car, same color lights, whizzed past me.

Mmmm, I thought, trouble on Washington Rd. I could only guess that the worst had happened and asked God to bless the people involved. It was later that day that I heard by radio of the accident at the intersection of Washington and Belair Roads, a spot I had just come through. God had safely navigated me around that site BEFORE the wreck. I was fine. I was safe. My husband, who has a grandstand seat to the traffic madness, told me later that there was a 4 or 5 car pileup, who could count? Probably where I would have been at the time.

God has a wonderful way of sheltering us. He loves us so much. He loves me. He loves you.

"You are my hiding place. You preserve me from trouble; you surround me with songs of deliverance." Psalm 32:7

"He that dwelleth in the secret place of the most high, shall abide under the shadow of the Almighty." Psalm 91:1

AT THE END OF THE RAINBOW

My favorite uncle had passed away. I fondly remembered the many hours we spent water skiing together. With my Dad driving the boat, my uncle and I would each pull up on one ski and ride the wake down Keg Creek. In the middle of the lake, I would kick off my ski and climb onto his shoulders. Hooking my feet under his arms, I hung down his back as we sped along. Oh to be 18 again!

He passed some 50 years after that and I know that he is in Heaven as I type this. My uncle was what you would call "jolly". He always had a laugh or a joke to tell. As it says in Proverbs 17:22 "A merry heart doeth good like a medicine, but a broken spirit drieth up the bones."

At the funeral, his celebration picture board recorded a full and busy life from fishing to successful business ventures.

On the back of the celebration bulletin, was printed the poem;

LOOK FOR ME IN RAINBOWS

"Time for me to go now, I won't say goodbye
Look for me in rainbows way up in the sky....."

I came home, feeling happy that he was free of the illness that bound him and sad that he was gone. I knew where he was though, as we are promised that every born-again child of God will be with Him. "To be absent from the body, is to be present with the Lord." II Corinthians 5:8

Back home, as I pondered over my uncle's life, I rounded the corner to my laundry room and stopped amazed in my tracks. There on that laundry room door was a RAINBOW. It isn't that I didn't know what was causing the rainbow. Our kitchen hutch is full of glass objects capable of creating such a sight. It was just that I HAD NEVER NOTICED IT UNTIL THAT NIGHT OF THE FUNERAL. Of course, I see it every night now. How did I never notice it before? I really can't say. God's timing is perfect.

"This is the sign of the covenant which I am making between Me and you and every living creature that is with you, for all successive generations. I set my bow in the cloud and it shall be for a sign of the covenant between me and the earth." Genesis 9:12-13

THE HOLY LAND EXPERIENCE

For several years, I had wanted to go to the Holy Land Experience in Orlando, Florida. Well, it was more of a very deep desire, not just a want. Since I've traveled quite a bit, but never to Israel, and since it is a small slice of Jerusalem and all the things I hold dear as a Christian, I was heart-drawn.

I asked many friends and relatives if they wanted to go with me, but schedules never quite meshed. I would sit at my computer for hours trying to work out the logistics of not having to drive there by myself. I live about 6 hours away — a long trip alone.

No, I also didn't want to fly down and rent a car because that would still be me driving alone in Orlando, a very busy attraction city. Could I fly in and get shuttled to the Holy Land? Nix on that; no one offers that service. I was virtually locked out.

Then I married my wonderful husband Marc, my modern-day Boaz (That's another awesome story written in my book SUDDENLY GOD). We had both lost our spouses, and after a 47-year friendship, God beautifully united us. And then the plot thickened.

We had a glorious wedding in May, 2011, and in July, Marc just casually mentioned that we would be vacationing at our timeshare in August.

" And where is that?" I asked.

"Oh, it's in Orlando," he replied.

I could almost hear angels singing in the background to the rhythm of my heart.

Needless to say, I have taken in the wonders of the Holy Land Experience twice now. The goodness of God always amazes me.

"Delight yourself in the Lord, and he will give you the desires of your heart." Psalm37:5

"If you, then being evil, know how to give good gifts to your children, how much more will our Father who is in heaven give what is good to those who ask Him!" Matthew 7:11

A PATCH JUST IN TIME

My deceased husband, Keith, was a truck driver, who traveled the 48 over-the- road states, wind in his hair. Although truck driving jobs are plentiful, for various reasons, one time, he didn't have one. We started to worry, which is never a good thing with God. Fear is a lack of faith and without faith, it is impossible to please God.(Hebrews 11:6).

I had been reading a lot of Bible seed time and harvest scriptures and the Holy Spirit impressed me to bury a truck job seed. I grabbed up a red and gold truck-decorated shirt patch , and carted it out to the backyard garden for burial. I know that sounds strange, but I have learned never to question the Holy Spirit, just to obey.

Smoothing the moist soil around the patch, I trusted God to sprout a job for my husband.

It wasn't long before that job seed bloomed right into a real job and all was well again. I had planted a patch and Keith had received a truck driving job. Exactly what was needed.

To make God's love more abundant — and it always is-the patch was planted for a new job and who was the new job with? Apache (A-patch-ee) Truck driving Company. Doesn't God have a wonderful sense of humor?

"Commit your work to the Lord, and your plans will be established." Proverbs 16:3

"Beloved, I wish above all things that you should prosper and be in good health, even as your soul prospers." 3 John 1:2

DANCE WITH JACK'S DOG

I was running late. If I hurried, I could grab a bite to eat and make it to my exercise class without losing my back corner spot at Silver Sneakers. We seniors are very adamant about "our spot". And besides I like it back there where no one can see me.

As I started down my short street, THERE HE WAS! Jack's huge Shetland-pony-size black and white dog was standing right in the middle of my street, attached to a 10-foot rope, obviously not hooked up anymore to where it should be. Only to Jake. I stopped the car with a jolt. Jake was standing right in front of me out on his own about 20 feet from a busy thoroughfare intersecting our quiet street. My neighbor is a great owner and this was indeed unusual.

I had a dilemma — stop and help or let Jake be found by his owner or worse yet, head out into the busy traffic and be with us no more.

First, I turned down Jack's winding driveway, hoping to alert him. I didn't have his phone number in my phone. Oh wonderful, I thought, Jake is following along with me back up to the house. Several long blows on my horn did not produce Jack. About this time, I was out of the car holding the 10-foot rope, at the end of which Jake was doing his happy dance, jumping wildly up and down. Still no response from Jack.

So then I called the next-door neighbor, whose number I DID have. I explained that I was on the way out and she volunteered to come over and see what she could do. But, instead, she called Jack and he popped out of his house and was very happy to see Jake, who had broken his rope and set out on his adventure alone. Tragedy averted.

Now I was late and 10 minutes behind where I should have been. No matter, we had probably saved Jake's life. I settled back in my still-running car and smiled as I heard the story playing on Christian radio of the Good Samaritan who had been the good neighbor and given of his time and money to save someone he didn't know. It made me feel that God was smiling back at me. And by the way, I WASN'T late for class — it just somehow all worked out.

"Love the Lord your God with all your heart and with all your soul and with all your strength and with all your mind and love your neighbor as yourself." Luke 10:27

"Then Jesus said to him 'Go and do the same.'" Luke 10:37

A LOT OF SLOTS

Don't ever loan or give away what you can't afford to lose. There is a great scripture (below) that lets us know, though, that the devil has to return 7 times what he steals from us.

A couple of years ago, a good friend borrowed $60 for some help with her great grandchild's medical bills.

I just expected it back when she had it, but a year went by and it didn't show up and that made me mad. Not so much with my friend, but with the devil for stealing from me. I was trying to be nice — but the devil, not so nice.

About that time, my husband, our daughter and I took a trip to Maine, which we do as often as we can (there are several trips to Maine in this book). After we spent a wonderful time exploring the beautiful coast, it was time to go back to Bangor Airport to return home.

It all happened because after driving two hours from the coast, we arrived in Bangor quite early for our flight home. The casino, located around the corner from the airport, enticed us and Marc, my husband, said," Ok, we can only stay an hour." Well, an hour is better than nothing, right? I took out $20 to play and also gave our daughter, Jessi, $20.

We all separated and I played several machines and then worked my way along the wall and sat down at an Eagle machine, not even necessarily my favorite machine. Not then, but it is now. I was playing $1 but then I decided I'd just play $2 at a time because the Leaping Lemons had been so good to me and it was almost time to go. Maybe the Eagles would fly home to nest too.

To my amazement, I won 55 free games. That's never before happened to me — sure, maybe 10 free games, but never 55. I was glad that I had just upped my bet to $2. The free plays kept spinning around and around. As did my head. I phoned my family, who was down a couple of rows, to get on over here so we could all watch and be astounded together. Security also arrived to make sure that machine was doing the right thing - 55 free spins is a lot! When the smoking machine got done, the haul was $474.80 — if my math is correct, that would include 7 x 60 plus $40 invested and a small bonus of $14.80 because God always does abundantly more than you ask or think. Payback.

When my friend finally did mention the loan, I was able to smile and say, "Hey, God has already taken care of that." Such a good feeling.

"People do not despise a thief if he steals to satisfy his appetite when he is hungry, but if he is caught, he will pay sevenfold." Proverbs 6:30

"A friend loves at all times." Proverbs 17:17

A WAY OF ESCAPE

It was many years ago, when my deceased truck driving husband, Keith, was bringing home $1 to $1000 weekly. True, as a state caseworker, I was paid every time, but   I never knew how much was coming in on Keith's checks, and became an expert in budgeting and paying bills on time. When you can't take care of your debts, a certain tension builds much like a pressure cooker, poised to go off at any time. Such was the day I parked in the dental college garage.

I had been reading God's thoughts on being under stress and loved this verse: "No temptation has overtaken you but such is common to man: and God is faithful, who will not allow you to be tempted beyond what you are able, but with the temptation will provide the way of ESCAPE also, so that you will be able to endure it." I Corinthians 10:13

Dentistry over, I walked back out to the garage and started up my little beige Colt. Down the row, I noticed someone backing out of their space and was waiting for them to stop and pull forward. Only they kept on backing and backing and backing. Now you would think under the circumstances, I would have quickly shifted into reverse to avoid the inevitable consequences. No, I didn't. I think that would have happened in the movies but I was just frozen in time when the solid thud hit the front of my almost paid-for car. One payment left.

We both hopped out and exchanged insurance information and names. Within a few days, I was holding a check for $1000, which came in very handy at the time. Checking on the car repair, I found that $250 would be sufficient to patch up my older car, so I set about planning the balance on what needed to be taken care of.

As I entered the department store where a payment was due, I fairly glided through toward customer service. My plan became not merely to pay the amount due, but to zero out the entire balance. Smiling, I turned the corner and the perfume counter caught my eye. The featured product was "ESCAPE."

My smile broadened and my heart beamed with thankfulness. God is able and He always shows us the way.

"Behold, I have graven thee on the palms of my hands." Isaiah 49:16

"I have loved you with an everlasting love. I have drawn you with unfailing kindness." Jeremiah 31:3

MY POSSESSED CAR

Time to go again to God's wonderful Jackson Hole, Wyoming, one of the places of my heart. I say I buy my snow in the Winter, because it rarely finds it's way to Georgia. And I do love snow! Not even two years living on the coast of Maine cured me of that. So each and every January, I fly on out to enjoy the overabundant snows of Wyoming. They have enough. They don't mind sharing.

It was Tuesday and I was busy getting things ready to leave on Thursday, when my PT Cruiser started acting up.(Now, I love my PT Cruiser. I bought one of the first ones and replaced it at 60,000 miles with another one just like it — same burgundy color and all) Why was my cherished car acting up and why at this time? THE BACK WINDOW WOULD NOT CLOSE. Well, although we were in the January thaw (from what, I have never figured out) in Georgia, still I would have to leave the possessed car at the airport while I was gone. Couldn't do that with the reluctant window down. I checked with a car serviceman friend and he said something like that was an electronic problem and that the car would have to be left for a day while the door was ripped apart and pondered over. No time to spare. I didn't have that kind of time.

Lord, I prayed, I really need this fixed and I don't know what to do.

I went to sleep, dreaming of staying at Snow King across from the ski lift and marveling at the skiers coming down the slope, pushing up powder all the way. It was 4 o'clock in the morning when I bolted up in bed.

"Try the second key."

I knew this was from the Holy Spirit because if I had known things like that, I would have used it earlier. You would have thought I'd run right out to the garage, but I snuggled back into the warmth of blankets and security and being well taken care of.

I DID jump up at 7 AM and race out to the garage with the second key. Car started right up and in my rear view mirror, I witnessed that back window sliding slowly to the top, completely closing itself. Problem solved, weigh lifted from shoulders.

Needless to say, Jackson Hole was extra glorious that year and I marveled at God's Mountains frosted in deep snow. Vacation was even better because I knew I was well taken care of and loved. That's just the way God is.

"Jesus looked at them and said, 'With man this is impossible, but with God all things are possible.'"
Matthew 19:26

"And my God will supply all your needs according to his riches in glory in Christ Jesus."
Philippians 4:19

BEST CHRISTMAS PRESENT EVER

It was Christmas, one of my favorite times of the year. Some people see it as a hassle and get all stressed out over shopping and planning their special event, but I glory in it. From the moment that lights twinkle and festooned trees appear in stores, I get a feeling that can't be explained. I am part kid waiting for Santa and part adult that knows the reason for the season. After all, it is the King of Kings' birthday. What a party! Jesus was sent by His Father, God, to redeem us from our sins and give us life abundant. That is really what THIS book is all about — abundant life. And that is exactly what the celebrations of Christmas and Easter remind me of.

And so, I was busy cooking a dish to take to my son's home. The mantle has been passed from my grandmother, to my Mother, to me, and now to my oldest son, and his wife. Christmas celebration lunch would be up the road at their beautiful, many-acre land with donkeys, atvs and a fishing pond — certainly the most fun place to have Christmas celebration.

As I was cooking, I grazed my pinkie finger across the burner. Oh ouch! (See, I'm not a great cook.) I could smell the scorching of my pinkie flesh and looked down to see that it was that awful white color. Not worth a trip to the emergency room on a Christmas Day, but still uncomfortable on this blessed day, a day meant to be filled with fun, family and laughter. And now, this pesky pain.

After a cold-water dousing of the throbbing finger, I sat down on the living room sofa to inspect the damage. Yep, burned to a crisp all right. Yep, it hurt something fierce. As I was pondering my emergency course of action, I could see the very lovely manger scene on the coffee table in front of me. I thought I felt the Holy Spirit impress me to just pick up the baby Jesus. That seemed weird, but after all, there IS healing in the name of Jesus.

"Just pick up the baby Jesus," the impulse came again.

I know it sounds bizarre; it sounded bizarre to me too. I had no choice but to comply. When I picked up the baby Jesus, the white spot faded and the pain was gone. I could hardly believe my eyes, but you know, God's still in the healing business and we don't give Him enough credit sometimes. All I know is I was hurting and then I wasn't. That was my best Christmas present ever!

"…by his wounds you have been healed." I Peter 2:24

"So do not fear, for I am with you; do not be dismayed for I am your God. I will strengthen you and help you, I will uphold you with my righteous right hand." Isaiah 41:10

THE ANGEL OF THE LORD

It was a sad time in my life many years ago, with lots of important decisions to make. Alone in my home, and sitting tearfully on my bed, I became aware of someone standing behind my right shoulder. As I turned to look, I could see a very huge being. My eyes traveled up the enormous gray almost statute-like form but I never saw his face. I don't know how that's possible, I just know that's the way it happened. Instantly, it felt like a very warm blanket was thrown over me. I would almost have to call it not only warm, but a blanket of peace embracing me. My heartache fled in that presence and I was able to see clearly through my decisions. God knew His plans for me.

God promised in the Bible, that angels are always there, caring for us, lifting us up and helping us in whatever we're going through. They are ministering spirits sent to render service for us – God's helpers in THE JOURNEY THROUGH this fallen world.

When Adam and Eve handed the keys over to Satan by eating from the forbidden tree and disobeying God, the earth took a spiral downward from which it hasn't yet recovered. Only the second coming of our Lord, Jesus Christ, can fix things up.

You, too, have this help. If we complain and whine, our angel stands quietly by, hands folded, and cannot be of service, they are required to act on God's words — the ones that He gave out when He created this earth. When we get with the "program" then the angels can be busily about bringing us the blessings that God wants us to have. If you give good gifts to your children, then think of how much more our Heavenly Father wants to bless His children. That would be you. That would be me.

Again, think of it like gravity. You can circumvent gravity but for a little bit — toss something into the air, blast something off with a powerful thrust, but always under its own devices, it is drawn back down to earth because that is the law God set up. It is the same with his word. Learn it, speak it and his helpers, the angels, will see that it comes to pass. DO NOT WORSHIP ANGELS. There are many scriptures that admonish us not to do this. Just appreciate them and give them something to work with by speaking scripture. Who knows, you may see yours. I was privileged to see mine only once so many years ago, but I praise God for that.

"Are they not all ministering spirits, sent forth to minister for them who shall be heirs of salvation?" Hebrews 1:14

"Bless the Lord, you His angels, you mighty ones who do his commandments, hearkening to the voice of His word." PS 103:20

THE SMASHING GIFT

I first went to Jackson Hole, Wyoming about 2000, I had always wanted to see the grandeur of Yellowstone, as everyone should, as it is our first National Park and spectacular. Since that first time, I have been so smitten, I have been back in Winter and Summer at least a dozen times. Watching the buffalo parade down the streets in Summer and strolling along the boardwalks around craters and geysers, seems "other worldly." I also go out in the Winter to get my snow fix when you can only snow coach into a small section of the park. I'm from Georgia and Wyoming always graciously shares snow with me. I think we all have places of the heart. Yellowstone is one of mine.

The January after my husband, Keith, passed away in November, my being just needed to be transported to that healing place.

I decided that since I didn't have all the affairs from my husband's death settled perhaps I'd better not make the trip that year. But I DID ASK God for extra money for the trip.

"Just send me something that I wasn't expecting — like found money," I said. He has a lot of that as he "owns all the cattle on a thousand hills." Psalm 50:10

I was sitting at a stop sign, waiting to pull out into traffic, when I felt the thud of another car wanting to be in the same place I was. I got out to assess the damage, as did the apologetic driver. At first I thought, no harm done, even though my bumper was really scratched up. Viewing the damage, I wasn't going to call the police, but then, in the back of my teenage years, I heard my Dad's voice that you should always make a report.

Surprisingly, I received a check for $1200.00 less than a week later, just enough for an airline ticket and hotel stay in Jackson Hole. Hmm, I thought, I really should use this to take care of a bill. But then I could almost hear God's voice say to me, "I beg your pardon. What did you ask me for?"

And so, on that wonderfully found money, I quickly purchased a trip to Jackson Hole and was doubly blessed by the gift God had given me. The bright sun laced snow seemed especially grand that year as I breathed in the goodness of God.

"He gives snow like wool." Psalm 147:16

"For every good and perfect gift is from above, and comes down from the Father of lights with whom there is no variation or shadow of turning." James 1:17

ROOTED IN GOD

I woke up early in wild anticipation of our trip to the Maine coast in just a few hours. While I was still snuggled under the covers, using up my last lounging moments, my tongue landed on a front-tooth crown and it seemed to be wiggling.

"Oh, no" I cringed, with that terrible sinking feeling in my stomach, "I'm going to lose a front tooth crown on the day I'm traveling 3 airplanes to the coast of Maine." If you've ever had dental problems, you know that dreadful feeling. And might I add, I've been in the dental chair almost every day of my life. I just have soft teeth.

I kept this to myself, not alerting my husband. There was nothing that could be done before travel time anyway.

On the way to the airport, we grabbed a biscuit and I fairly shredded it and shoved it into the back of my mouth, avoiding the wiggly area.

Bags checked and security over, we walked down the long hallway in our small airport. IT WAS THEN THAT I SAW IT! I glanced up and the John Deere advertisement almost blinded me. It was complete with live tractor, and read, "Rooted in the CSRA." (thats the Central Savannah River Area where we live).

The Holy Spirit then spoke to my heart, and while it might not make any sense to anyone else, as these things sometimes don't, I felt His assurance that there would be no problem with that well-ROOTED tooth on our trip.

And so there wasn't, not for that week nor has there been this 5 months later.

How very precious of God to ease my fears so that I could enjoy my vacation on the beautiful Maine coast with my husband. He always has that warm comforting embrace for all of us.

"The Lord your God is with you, He is mighty to save. He will take great delight in you, He will quiet you with His love, He will rejoice over you with singing." Zephaniah 3:17

"Blessed be the God and Father of our Lord Jesus Christ, the Father of mercies and God of all comfort." 2nd Corinthians 1:3

THE LAST AND THE FIRST DAY

It was 2010 and Marc and I had known each other for 46 years as God wove our tapestries around each other. I knew but Marc didn't. (See my book SUDDENLY GOD for the whole beautiful story)

When I say I "knew," it was one day when Marc hugged me at his business that God whispered in my ear. He had lost his wife a year before and I was still struggling with a husband who had long since moved into the bedroom across the hall and made himself unavailable after many years of marriage. He also was in very failing health. He had lost one leg, as had Marc's wife before she passed away, and I was in Marc's store seeking advice for the same condition with my husband. He had all the answers and could tell me exactly what to do and expect. We were acquaintances and then friends gathered under the same umbrella of grief and bewilderment that these things cause.

My husband DID pass away right before Thanksgiving, but it had not yet been published in the paper. I was at lunch with my daughter and her family the day before Thanksgiving. Of all the times we could have eaten at the little corner neighborhood restaurant and of all the booths to be assigned, where I was sitting, I was facing out towards the door.

I glanced up and saw him standing there, searching for his family he was lunching with. I gasped, and said to my daughter, "There's Marc."

I rushed up to meet him, spilling out the story of Keith's death, over my sobs. Marc hugged and hugged and hugged me and I thought he would not let go — ever. He said to me much later that it was then he knew. But he didn't act on this at all.

We hugged in greeting at church after that (As you can probably guess by now, Marc is a great hugger. His embrace is like a big warm teddy bear) and it was 3 months later that I made the decision to come to Marc's church, where I had been for a while, one last time. It was too hard. I said nothing to him or anyone about what God had whispered to me. I and I alone knew. He didn't know that this would be my last day gazing up at him from the back row as his song rang out from the choir.

As friends we had talked several times about going to the gorgeous, historical Biltmore House in Asheville, NC. I had decided to go that February 2011 and as Marc approached me that morning, smiling and making the long trip to the back of the church, knowing this was a now-or- never moment, because I wasn't coming back, I casually said:

"I'm going to the Biltmore this month, do you still wanna to go?"

He had no idea that this was my last contact with him. God knows the plans He has for us.

I almost fell over at his response,

"Yes," he exclaimed, without missing a beat "and my Mom and daughter aren't here today – I'll come back and sit with you after the choir sings, and oh yes, are you staying for the lunch after church?"

"No, I hadn't planned to" — but he said," I wish you would and you can sit with me."

It was a while before I could breathe. First nothing and then all of this in one breath — whew. Good thing he had to go back to the choir so I could collect myself. God might tell you what the plans are, but he doesn't tell you, you could fall over when they come to pass. I stayed for lunch with Marc and from then on, I was gathered under his wing.

We haven't been apart since then. We're married 6 years now and I'll always remember how he held my hand all the way as we drove to Asheville-a good 3-hour trip from where we live in Georgia. What was to be my last contact with Marc wasn't the last but only the beginning – God knows the plans He has for us. He is always on time.

"For I know the plans I have for you, declares the Lord, plans to prosper you and not to harm you, plans to give you hope and a future." Jeremiah 29:11

"I will sing of the lovingkindness of the Lord forever." Psalm 89:1

THE TOOTH ANGEL

I was experiencing some issues with my teeth, as sometimes happens when we get older, and already was wearing a small partial on the bottom. I like eating, so I was doing whatever it took to continue that great activity.

The partial proved comfortable and provided just what I needed. But I also wanted some back molars in empty spaces on top. The appliance was ordered and came back with a metal roof. It was horrifying and after several attempts, I just didn't want to wear it. Metal is very foreign in my mouth. It felt like a small planet had come to roost there.

And so it was on a Thursday that I visited my oral surgeon and asked the question.

"Do I have to wear metal in my mouth? Is there another option?"

Keep in mind that I have several implants and several other implants had failed, thus my relationship with this very kind oral surgeon who removed the failing implants done by someone else. That dreadful metal appliance had also been done by someone else.

"Well, he said, I just read about a flexible appliance."

It was not something that he took care of, but something that he could recommend. The question was where to go for this appliance.

Keep in mind, for this story's sake, that was Thursday. I kept thinking on that more magical appliance and it was on Saturday, just two days later, that my husband, son and I lunched at a local restaurant.   TWO DAYS LATER. I excused myself and went into the lady's room to rinse my comfortable lower appliance.

Just at that time, a lady came bounding out of the stall and there I stood.

"I'm sorry," I said, "embarrassed that she had to see me, partial in hand."

"Oh, don't worry about it," she said, and immediately whipped an appliance out of her mouth.

IT WAS THE COVETED FLEXIBLE UPPER APPLIANCE! TWO DAYS LATER!

I quickly began asking questions about comfort and flexibility and she pinched that thing right together. We shared a moment in that restroom. Was she a woman or was she an angel God sent to counsel me? I don't know. I'm just grateful she showed up.

I have the flexible partial now and it works wonderfully well — that is, until God replaces my teeth — which He can do you know. Such a reminder that He so cares about us in whatever we are going through.

"Cast all your care upon Him because he cares for you." I Peter 5:7
"If you ask me anything in my name, I will do it." John 14:14

WORKING FOR JESUS

It was 1979 and a hard time in my life. I had relocated my 3 kids, 3 cats and a dog to Maine, a place of my heart, to a large Victorian house, overlooking the chilly waters of Penobscot Bay. After selling my educational childcare business in Atlanta, I had set out to get quiet and seek God. There was a wonderful small gazebo off my bedroom where I enjoyed Penobscot's waves and did my writing.

Although I had several small incomes, there was never enough to keep up with the growing demands of my little family. Child support and proceeds from my sale came in small monthly dribbles. When my job teaching an autistic child ended abruptly in the Summer, I decided to rent out one of the bedrooms in that big house as my children were down south for the Summer thing with Grandmother and Dad. I had no idea that a job wouldn't just unfold for me in that small seacoast town, although I had several strong job talents and sent out many resumes.

I obtained only one interview from that large batch of resumes and went in with confidence that I could become the next Assistant to the Special Ed teacher. Although I possessed no degree, I did have 3 years of college in Child Psychology and Education and had worked with children for a number of years in my school. My college campus days had consisted of nights only. I was married and just kept having babies, although a doctor had assured me that wasn't possible. Well, fool him. Therefore, I consider my 3 children special miracles. But it was getting tough to continue caring for small children, managing my house and doing homework. Getting pregnant the third time was the last straw as far as keeping up with that crazy schedule. I withdrew from class and thus, that's the reason I didn't and still don't have a degree. But God uses me in spite of that. (After 8 years of night classes in between diapers, I felt I should have been awarded a PhD. Well, not really.)

Several weeks later the dreaded letter showed up in my mailbox-"we have chosen someone else," it fairly screamed at me.

So thus, I did rent out one of the 5 bedrooms for the Summer to a NICE young man. Or so I thought. He moved his girlfriend in almost immediately, causing a conversation about extra electricity and water that I really didn't want to have (they entertained a lot and I wasn't affluent that year). We struck a deal. Because the owners wanted their wonderful Victorian house back in the Fall, my little family had to move out and I found a suitable 100-year-old house down to Rockport, overlooking the pier where Andre the Seal lived. I certainly needed a truck and helping hand to move. My tenant had such a truck so the deal we struck was for him to move us with his vehicle come Fall when we all had to vacate the premises.

It didn't happen. At departure time, he let me down by saying he just didn't have to help me. You know, sometimes people act that way. At that time, I had only $200 in my checking account.

I prayed, "Lord, I surely need help."

Fortunately, my new landlord found someone willing to move us over for that exact amount. Wouldn't you know? $200. Now I had no money, no job and my kids were due back home.

I walked despondently to the mailbox trying to work up a plan. The kids were coming and I have hungry kids. But just on that very low day, a letter from the Maine Public School system showed up in my box.

"We want you, we want you!" it sang.

The chosen candidate had to decline.

"Can you come?"

Could I come? I could come there with bells on. God is always on time. We moved, my kids came back and I went to work well taken care of by my Father all in the same week. And oh yes, God is always abundant. The kids had plenty to eat.

"I once was young and now I am old but I have not seen a righteous person forsaken or his descendants begging for bread." Psalm 37:25-26

"And God is able to make all grace abound to you, so that always having all sufficiency in everything, you may have an abundance for every good deed." 2 Corinthians 9:8

MY COOL BIRTHDAY

I live in the very hot South and during the Summer, could dine outside by frying eggs on the sidewalk. Well, I wasn't born here – I was born at Flower Fifth Avenue Hospital in Manhattan, New York (true story — but lest you get too impressed, it was a charity hospital at the time). I think my body has been trying to get cooler ever since I came back South by train with my Mother and sister when the New York Experiment, as well as my Mother's marriage, had failed.

As a two-year old, asleep on a suitcase on my way back to Georgia, I didn't have a say in the matter. My Mother and Father had left their roots in Jesup, Georgia, where my Great Grandfather had grown the first Georgia tobacco crop on his farm, to find their fortune in the Big City. They didn't and they also lost each other.

I'm telling you all of this to let you know that my June 14th (Flag Day) birthday is sizzling hot and I always long for a cool one. Why can't I be wearing a wool hat and scarf, romping in birthday snow?

Last birthday, I prayed to God that I could have a temperature of 83 degrees with rain, knowing how utterly impossible that was in the blazing Summer South. But hey, God can do the impossible. Why ask for something simple?

When I got up on June 14th, the Weather Channel scrolled the temperature range of 74/97. The day got hotter and hotter and hotter. Still there was grocery shopping to be done. As I rolled my purchased groceries from the store out to the car, I could feel perspiration sliding down my face. We Southern ladies don't like to sweat. Yucky, yucky. Sometimes we go in May and come out in October. I rode home, eying a canopy of accumulating clouds, dreading the hot dragging of groceries out of the car and into the house.

Chores done, I finally sat down in my fortunately air-conditioned cool house. It was 4:00 pm. The temperature held steady at 97 degrees.

About an hour later, I watched in wonder as the wind picked up and a sheet of rain swept over my yard. At least a little heat relief. I thought, Oh ye of little faith. I'm going to tell you, and I have a picture of this, that at 5:11 in the afternoon, it was 83 degrees and raining. It wasn't 82 and it wasn't 84 degrees. It was 83 and raining at 5:11 pm — the hottest part of the day in Evans, Ga. Happy Birthday to me from God.

"Ask and it will be given to you...."Matthew 7:17

"Ask rain of the Lord at the time of the Spring rain." Zechariah 10:1

FIRST YOU SEE IT AND THEN YOU DON'T

I was at our neighborhood movie theater, where I longed to be when I worked full time and just was able to get there as I wove it around raising kids and working. Now that I am retired, I can go whenever I want. And I do.

I really like climbing up to the top row in the center with my popcorn, coke and candy, and I actually like it when there is no one else in there with me. It's therapy for me. This was such a day.

After seeing a wholesome movie (I don't go above PG-13 rating because I don't think the Holy Spirit, who lives inside me, would enjoy it and I'm even selective about those.), I came out and blinked in the bright sunlight of Summer. I walked over to the parking lot edge where I always leave my 2007 Burgundy PT Cruiser and to my astonishment, there was nothing there.

Okay, okay, maybe I parked in a different spot because, if it looks like rain, I occasionally do that. Now I am pacing up and down rows of cars pushing my keypad panic button — pushing and then listening. I heard nothing; I saw nothing. One last push. Still only silence. I wanted to cover all my bases before my alarm call to my husband, Marc.

"Honey," I tried to calmly say, "I'm over in the movie parking lot and my car is gone."

"What?" he said. "Is this a joke?"

It was then that the situation caught up with and overwhelmed me-

"WOULD I JOKE ABOUT A THING LIKE THIS!" I shouted into the phone.

Fortunately, our business is just down the street and my husband finally took me seriously

"God, I said, "please find my car for me."

The sun was beating down on me. I was getting hot; I was getting sweaty Southern women don't like to sweat. Yucky, yucky.

In no time, my husband, who had ripped his car out of the hands of the detailer at his tire and auto store, came roaring up and I threw myself around his neck. He and I stared puzzled at the empty spot where my car used to be, letting the reality sink in. Who would want a 2007 PT Cruiser, except me. I love my car. It's actually my second burgundy PT Cruiser and they don't make them anymore. Good thing I'm married to a tire and auto repair shop. I wanted to drive it forever before it went missing.

"Did you look through the parking lot?" Such a husband thing to say.

"YES, OF COURSE!" I shouted.

Before we could take any action, call the police or the swat team, up pulled a wrecker with my car riding like a princess on its trailer.

Oh, my gosh. Thank you Jesus. No police, no juveniles going to the Youth Detention Center, no car stashed in the river. No problem. It took a few minutes to process as we drank what was going on.

"I thought I saw you pulling past my store," my husband said.

"Yep" the driver said sheepishly. "When I went to deliver her, they said, hey, not our car. So I had to bring her back."

Before we could call the police or get really crazy, she came waltzing back up. Problem solved. Isn't God good?

If I had been a few minutes later coming out of the movies, my car would have been safely returned to its spot and I would have never known, You never know what your car is doing while you're in the movies. But God did.

"In my trouble, I cried to the Lord, and He answered me." Psalm 120:1

"I will lift up mine eyes unto the hills, from whence cometh my help. My help cometh from the Lord, who made Heaven and earth." Psalm 121:1,2

ABOUT THE AUTHOR

Geraldine Yount is retired from Family and Children's Services, where she worked for 24 years. She also owned and operated an educational child care center in Atlanta, Georgia. She now lives in the Augusta, GA area with her husband, Marc. The beautiful marriage that God planned for them continues. In 2016, she published *Suddenly God,* which tells their story. It is available in print and Kindle.

She has also written several children's values series books under the name Geraldine Alexander Stockham, and these are entitled *The Purple Trouble* and *The Big Bold Lie.* They are paperback and can be purchased through Amazon.com.

53956599R00017

Made in the USA
Columbia, SC
25 March 2019